OFF THE COUCH

OFF THE COUCH

Noé Marchevsky

Translated from Portuguese
Ruth G. Kirstein

KARNAC

Published in 2003 by Karnac Books Ltd.
118 Finchley Road, London NW3 5HT

This edition is based on *No Divã do Dr. Fritz* published by Casa do Psicólogo São Paulo in 2001

British Library Cataloguing in Publication Data

A C.I.P. for this book is available from the British Library

ISBN 9781855759442

Edited, designed, and produced by The Studio Publishing Services Ltd.

Printed in Great Britain

www. karnacbooks.com

To Maria

ACKNOWLEDGEMENTS

I would like to thank two very special persons: my cousin Mauricio Jose and my friend Sonia Zyngier.

Mauricio Jose Marchevsky is an architect and artist. With his help, this book, which initially existed only in my mind, gradually became a reality. Thanks to him, I acquired graphic parameters, something essentially new to me.

Sonia Zyngier, my dear friend, has revised many of my writings, including this book. She is a Professor of Stylistics and Literatures in English at the Federal University of Rio de Janeiro. With her magic touch, she transforms merely comprehensible texts into elegant ones.

To both, my gratitude!

ABOUT THE AUTHOR

Noé Marchevsky is a medical doctor and a Training Analyst of the Brazilian Psychoanalytic Society of Rio de Janeiro. He is also a member of the International Psychoanalytical Association.

His publications include 'Diagnostic Interviews with Adolescent and his Family' in *Técnica Psicoterápica na Adolescência* (1994) compiled by Roberto Graña, Editora Artes Médicas Sul Ltda; *Psychoanalysis in Practice* (1995) by Imago Editora; 'Interpretation and Therapeutic Actuality in Child Analysis' in *Atualidade da Psicanálise de Crianças* (2001), compiled by Roberto Graña, Casa do Psicólogo Editora.

A PRACTICAL COMPARATIVE STUDY OF MODELS OF INTERPRETATION IN DIFFERENT SCHOOLS OF PSYCHOANALYTIC THOUGHT

In order to demonstrate clearly the differences in the many schools of psychoanalytic thought, I selected a very simple statement which will be interpreted by some of my colleagues.

A very short sentence.

The patient, a young woman, arrives at the office and says:

"YESTERDAY I FINALLY HAD SEX WITH PETE!"

THAT'S ALL.

Don't be fooled, however, by the apparent simplicity of the statement, for secret feelings and mysterious messages are hidden in it and only psychoanalysts are able to understand them and interpret them. That depends, of course, on the theory that each one follows.

SHOULD WE START?   COME THIS WAY!

1. Techno-explanatory/topographic Freudian

DO YOU KNOW WHAT HAPPENED? YOU SUSPENDED
THE REPRESSION OF YOUR SUPER-EGO, THUS
LIBERATING THE ENERGY OF YOUR ID, AND THIS
TIME WITH A LESS AMBIVALENT EGO

Beginning around 1923, this model is still very much in use,
since it sounds learned and, when spoken in a firm and
authoritative voice, it creates a good impression. Much used
by young analysts.

2. Frightened Freudian

Theory used when the analyst (who obviously is the centre of the universe) believes that the patient did something stupid just as a reaction to the conflicts he has with him, the analyst.

3. Freudian of the type "Unhappy, hysterical and submissive women without a penis"

WELL, SALOME, FINALLY YOUR
PENIS ENVY HAS DECREASED!

Archaic, though still tempting! Some women may consider this an aggressive statement. However, followers of this group have developed subtle forms of constantly reaffirming that women, poor things, are castrated—and most men are, too.

4.   Post-hypnotic Freudian

I WILL TOUCH YOUR FOREHEAD
AND YOU WILL TELL ME THE FIRST
THOUGHT TO CROSS YOUR MIND

Pre-historic. Should be used only when the psychoanalyst
understands nothing and wishes, for heaven's sake, to obtain
some free association, and doesn't know how to ask for it.

5. A La Carte Transferential
Also known as Automatic Transferential

YOU ARE TELLING ME THAT IN YESTERDAY'S SESSION
WE ESTABLISHED A VERY INTIMATE RELATIONSHIP!

For some, a tranferential interpretation is the one that sees all
that is said by the patient as a parable, that in fact everything
involves the analyst. In order to use the automatic transference
interpretation, all you need to do is change the main characters
and the setting of the narrative to the analyst and his office.
Very simple. The only problem is that the patient sometimes gig-
gles. Be aware that the transferential interpretation entails
some risks and its formulation is important. It is very important
to make it clear that any form of intimacy happened "during our
session" (thus, symbolically); the analyst's statement should
always start with "You are telling me ..." so that the patient
will not think that the analyst is making anything up. The
responsibility of saying such things falls on the patient.

6. Jealous Transferential

SO YOU PREFERRED TO "DO IT"
WITH PETE RATHER THAN "DOING IT"
HERE IN MY OFFICE?

It occurs with insecure analysts.

7. Non-Transferential

AND WAS IT ANY GOOD?

Dangerous approach, which opens unexpected doors in the doctor–patient relationship. One does not know where this kind of talk may lead. To be on the safe side, it should only be used by very experienced professionals – those who are very self-assured—or impotent.

8. The Quickie Kleinian

SEE, YOU LITTLE FOOL, NOTHING MUCH HAPPENED. NONE OF YOUR SADISTIC FANTASIES MATERIALIZED. IT WAS ALL FANTASY! IN THE END, EVERYONE SURVIVED!

In just a few words, the Kleinian analyst makes his message clear: the patient, who hasn't even suspected it, is a sadistic, foolish, delirious person.

9.   Official Kleinian

THIS RELATIONSHIP WAS POSSIBLE ONLY BECAUSE YOUR AMOROUS/PROJECTIVE IDENTIFICATIONS FILLED PETE WITH GOOD THINGS AND YOU REINTROJECTED THE PENIS, YOUR MILK AND BABIES, ALL EQUIVALENT TO THE GOOD BREAST, SO YOU FEEL INTEGRATED!

It is implicit that the patient, at that moment, was in the depressive position, and the analyst, at that moment, was extremely generous.

10. Impatient Kleinian

This interpretation will only be understood if the patient is in a schizo-paranoid position.

11. Skeptical Kleinian

The psychoanalyst is sure her patient is divided, infantile, and delirious. She hasn't even learned how to symbolize, so how can she know what a penis is and what having sex is.

12. Kleinian using Projective Identification

TO HAVE SEX, TWO PERSONS ARE NEEDED.
YOU ARE TOTALLY MINGLED WITH PETE,
SO YOU ARE TOTALLY MISTAKEN.
YOU DIDN'T HAVE SEX WITH PETE AT ALL!

Patients with pretentious and arrogant statements can irritate a Kleinian.

13.   Ill-tempered Kleinian

BUT WHAT A TERRIBLE THING, MS. BENEDICT!
YOU ENDED UP DESTROYING EVERYTHING!
ARE YOU HAPPY NOW?
YOU ALLOWED YOUR NARCISSISTIC AND
ENVIOUS ASPECT TO TAKE OVER YOUR LIFE
AND KILL YOUR FUTURE.
YOU DESTROYED PETE AND YOURSELF, YOU DESTROYED
YOUR FAMILY, **YOU ATTACKED YOUR ANALYSIS!**
ISN'T THAT SO, MS. BENEDICT?

It is said that the ill-tempered Kleinian psychoanalyst can be
dangerous.

14. Impact Bionian (6.3 in the Richter scale)

YOU ARE TALKING ABOUT YESTERDAY'S RELATIONSHIP WITH PETE SO AS NOT TO TALK ABOUT TODAY'S RELATIONSHIP WITH ME

Said in a quiet tone of voice, it can be disconcerting to the patient. The analyst is triumphant and has his revenge because the patient is having pleasure with somebody else.

15. Objective Bionian

YESTERDAY, MS. ROSEMOND?
WHAT IS YESTERDAY?
WHAT ARE YOU TALKING ABOUT?
YESTERDAY DOES NOT EXIST!

Perceptive, indirect, and complicated way for a Bion follower to suggest that he'd rather speak about today, preferably about the present moment of the session.

16. Cosmic Bionian

THE SPACES OF THE BLACK HOLE OF YOUR GENITAL UNIVERSE TOUCH ORBITING, PENETRATING SATELLITE ELEMENTS IN PETE WHICH, THROUGH THIS ENCOUNTER, ARE TRANSFORMED, OEDIPALLY, INTO THE DISCOVERY OF THE ALREADY-KNOWN!

These tend to be beautiful interpretations. Sometimes it is even possible to get the meaning (which is not important). What really counts is the atmosphere.

17.   Superior Bionian

When said with a superior air, it totally exposes the patient who, even though she does not have the faintest idea what beta is, feels she is unable to outwit the analyst.

18. Mythological–Paralysing Bionian

FALLACIOUS PERSPECTIVES
APPROACH UNATTAINABLE MYTHS

A good way to paralyse the patient's mind; she won't be able to think for six months.

19. Self-Psychology Follower

The analyst will then write a paper describing how he treated and cured the patient's narcissism.

20. Erudite Self-Psychology Follower

THE SELF SPECULAR IMAGE OF SELF-OBJECT PETE
TRANSMITTED COHESION AND STABILITY TO YOUR
OWN SELF, AND HIS PENIS, FILLING THE VOID,
RAISED YOUR SELF-ESTEEM

The interpretation improves both the patient's and the
analyst's self-esteem.

21. Love Story
Self-Psychology Follower

YOU ARE OK!
YOU HAVE BEEN MAKING SUCH PROGRESS!
YOU HAVE BEEN FINDING SO MANY IMPORTANT THINGS
IN LIFE. YOU ARE CERTAINLY DESTINED TO BE HAPPY.
I AM AMAZED AND PROUD OF YOU!

At this moment, patient and analyst fall in love.

22.   Transitional Winnicottian

Winnicott followers know that their patients go through life attached to their transitional objects.

23.   Outpatient Winnicottian

YOU HAD SEX WITH PETE?
YOU LEARNED TO PLAY WITH HIS PENIS, IS THAT RIGHT?
GOOD! VERY GOOD! AND IF YOU USED YOUR TRUE SELF
AND IF LOVEMAKING WAS GOOD ENOUGH,
WE CAN SCHEDULE AN APPOINTMENT
FOR NEXT YEAR AT THIS SAME TIME!

This can be used in any government outpatient facility.

24. Objective Lacanian

FINALLY YOU MIRROR THE OBJECT-REVERSE OF THE LAW OF THE FATHER! EMPTY WORDS AND CASTRATED PHALLIC OBJECTS NEVER BECOME FULFILLED. THE SUBJECT OF SYMBOLIC KNOWLEDGE TRANSFERS THE REAL FROM THE IMAGINARY, TRANSFORMING FANTASMATIC REFLEXIVE SIGNIFYING OBJECTS INTO AN IMAGINARY SUBJECT OF THE REFLECTED SIGNIFIED

Of course!

25.   Offended Lacanian

26. Logical Lacanian

YOU HAD SEX?
OK, BUT OUR TIME IS UP!

"Logic time" was a revolutionary invention in psychoanalysis. The psychoanalyst no longer needs an appointment book.

27. Lacanian in a rare moment of doubt

LET'S MAKE IT CLEAR! WHO, AFTER ALL, HAD
SEX WITH PETE? **YOU OR ME?**
WAS IT A FULL ACT OR AN EMPTY ACT?
FANTASMATIC OR REAL?
OH, MY GOD! WAS IT REFLEXIVE?
WHOSE PENIS WAS IT, AFTER ALL?

Analysts also suffer from excruciating doubts.

28. Wishful Lacanian

THE SUBJECT OF YOUR
DESIRE'S DESIRE SATISFIES
THE DESIRE OF MY
DESIRING YOUR DESIRE

Desire must be placed somewhere.

29. Specular/Existential Lacanian

> VAST SPECULAR WORLD!
> MYS-TER-IOUS SUBJECT-OBJECT!
> YOU-PETE: PETE-YOU!
> IT'S NOT ME WHO IS HERE!
> **WHERE ARE WE?**

A Lacanian does not take part in the analytic process. He is a neutral being (not to be confused with sexually neutral), a type of oracle who uses hermetic language—just the way he learned it in the original texts.

30. Signifying Lacanian

IT WAS THE TRIUMPHANT PENETRATION
OF THE SIGNIFIER IN THE SIGNIFIED, THUS
SOLIDIFYING THE ILLUSION OF THE IMAGINARY

Deep down, this is similar to a Bionian, who would put it this way: "Nothing but the introduction of the contained into the container. And we hope it leads to alpha and not to an attack against the bond".
A Kleinian would say: "Your lovemaking is merely a manic attempt at reparation".
And the Self-follower would say that the patient was clearly better.

31.   Cognitive-Behaviourist

ISN'T PETE THAT DYKE
WHO LIVES UPSTAIRS?

Straightforward, simple, and objective: American.

32. Methodical Cognitive-Behaviourist

Nothing like good old pragmatism.

33. Primal Scream

Release the lion in you. If there is no lion in you, release
whatever ...

34. Therapist for Adolescents

36. Non-Interventionist

AND WHAT DO **YOU** THINK OF THAT?

37. Somewhat Non-Interventionist

I UNDERSTAND ...

38. Total Non-Interventionist

39. Poet Psychoanalyst

OH, HOW BEAUTIFUL!
DON'T SAY ANYTHING ELSE!
I'LL CREATE A POEM ...
SEMEN-SEED IN THE BUSHES, RAINING
BEAUTIFUL NIGHTS OF SUDDEN STRAINING!

Poetry-flavoured psychoanalysis.

40. French Punning School

LET'S EXAMINE YOUR STATEMENT:
YESTERDAY FINALLY …
FINE-ALLEY?
OK TO HAVE SEX IN THE ALLEY?
AND WHO IS FINALLY YOUR ALLY?
PETE OR ME?

This school of thought defends the idea that the secret
meaning of communication is hidden—guess where?—in the
words themselves. All you have to do is deconstruct them and
everything becomes clear.

41.   French Punning School Au Complet

A) Mechanism to understand the material:

Yes-ter-day
Yes = affirmation
ter = transliteration of tear, destroy
day = the present date

Fin-ally
Fin = dorsal appendix of some fishes
Ally = someone on your side

I had sex
I = that's myself!
had = to possess, own
SEX = that's the real thing!

with peter: With = that means I was not alone at that moment
Pe = pee - what you do after you drink a lot of fluid
ter (same as above)

B) INTERPRETATION:

AT THE PRESENT DATE I WILL, WITH THE DETERMINATION OF A SHARK, TRY TO BE ON YOUR SIDE, SO AS TO BE ABLE TO POSSESS THE URINE THAT REALLY MATTERS TO YOU BEFORE YOU TRY TO DESTROY IT!

42. The 'Joyeuse' version of the French School

The French always understood the importance of the body.

43. Psychoanalyst with an Administrative Function

THE UNEXPECTED INTRODUCTION OF THIS RIGID MATTER INTO YOUR FORMERLY VIRTUAL SPACE FAVOURS PROFOUND STRUCTURAL CHANGE. WE SHOULD BE OPEN TO NEW VENTURES. HOWEVER, WE DO HAVE TO SET LIMITS AND CHECK THE COST EFFECTIVENESS OF THE ENTERPRISE. IT WOULD BE BETTER TO ASK YOUR PARENTS AND THE IPA

This is the type of interpretation that occurs to those with titles such as President of the Psychoanalytic Society, Director of the Institute, etc.

44. All schools of thought

HUM-HUM ...

Often, this is the best thing to say, or rather, to whisper. The patient understands it as "I am here listening to you and I understand you perfectly well." Isn't it wonderful?

45. Free Association of the Analyst

PETE?
PETER-PAUL?
JOHN-PAUL?
JOHN-PAUL II?
IT SEEMS TO ME THAT
YOU ARE AFTER
A MYSTICAL
RELATIONSHIP!

This is an 'impromptu' analyst. The patient merely provides the theme and the interpretation depends on inspiration. Some patients become fascinated, not noticing the basic mistake that the free association should be made by the patient, not the therapist.

46. Mystical Psychoanalyst (there are some!)

SURE, **I KNEW IT**!
I KNEW IT VERY WELL!
YESTERDAY AT AROUND 3 PM
A WHITE DOVE PERCHED ON
MY WINDOWSILL.
IT LOOKED AT ME AND COOED.
AT THAT MOMENT
I WAS SURE
THAT YOU HAD HAD SEX!

There is a level of extra sensorial perception and communication that only a select few can reach.

47.   Psychosomatic

HOORAY! NO MORE ASTHMA, HIVES, OR HYSTERICAL PALSIES. **FROM NOW ON ORGASMS ONLY!**

48. Analyst who is observing babies

After writing down all details, you put your notebook in a drawer to create a report in the distant future.

49. A second-year student of psychoanalysis
First case in supervision

EVERY TIME YOUR MOTHER TRAVELS,
YOU BECOME ANXIOUS AND MAKING SOME SHRIMP
FRITTERS IS A WAY OF BRINGING HER BACK

This has nothing to do with the clinical material, but it was
used in the previous supervision class.

50. **During a Clinical Seminar**
Second-year student

Well, I think the patient is depressed, right? I mean, I felt the patient was depressed when she said that. Very depressed. In any case that is what I felt. What is important is what we feel, isn't it? The Oedipus complex. The imaginary. Attaining desire ... Don't you think? Freud spoke about that. Something reactive, manic. How come she suddenly had sex? There has to be an explanation. The imaginary must have taken hold. The mother isn't even mentioned. Did you notice? There is something missing. Things don't happen just like that, you know! I do not believe in coincidences. Why did she talk about that? Don't you think? It sounded like denial to me. I read that Freud said that repression leads to hysteria. I had a similar case. A nurse who didn't like to have sex; she imagined that she was taking a train trip. That was the only way she got aroused. But it was not just any train, it had to be the Orient Express. This having sex—that's very symbolic. Cases like that tend to have a lot of projection or projective identification. I don't quite know the difference between the two. In such cases the analyst has to be very careful. How old is the patient? 18 only? Ah, well, I thought she was around 20. That changes things quite a bit. There must be some symbiosis in the case and it is important to pay attention to countertransference. That is the most important thing in therapy. How did the patient put it? What was the atmosphere like during the session? This is very condensed material, isn't it? It is hard to know what she is talking about—just like this, suddenly! It sounds like a dream. Very hermetic, don't you think? Could you please read the material again?

51. Reichian

Direct and very pleasant method for the removal of armouring or inhibitions.

52. Group Psychotherapy

FOLKS, LET'S HAVE A HAND FOR OUR
COLLEAGUE WHO HAD SEX WITH PETE!

53. Jungian

ROMEO AND JULIET,
EROS AND PSYCHE,
ABELARD AND HELOISE,
PETE AND ROSEMARY ...
THE DESTINY IS ACCOMPLISHED!

54. Prophetic Jungian

AND SO HUMANITY PERPETUATES ...
BUT, BY ANY CHANCE, DID YOU
USE A CONDOM?

Collectively, right now, thousands of women around the world are unconsciously having sex with their Pete (and we are waiting for our turn).

SORRY FOR INTERRUPTING
BUT OUR TIME IS UP!